A Squirrel's Story
A True Tale

by
Jana Bommersbach

Illustrated by Jeff Yesh

Great Books for Growing Minds
A division of Five Star Publications, Inc.
Chandler, Arizona

Linda F. Radke, President
Five Star Publications, Inc.
PO Box 6698
Chandler, AZ 85246-6698
480-940-8182
www.FiveStarPublications.com

www.SquirrelsStory.com

Publisher's Cataloging-In-Publication Data

Bommersbach, Jana.
	A squirrel's story : a true tale / by Jana Bommersbach ; illustrated by Jeff Yesh.

	p. : col. ill. ; cm.

	Summary: The true story of Shirlee Squirrel and her children, this book provides a glimpse into the world of gray tree squirrels. Complete with factual information and important life lessons, including strengths within oneself.

	Interest age level: 004-010.
	Issued also as an ebook.
	ISBN: 978-1-58985-252-5

	1. Gray squirrel--Juvenile literature. 2. Ability--Juvenile literature. 3. Self-esteem--Juvenile literature. 4. Gray squirrel. 5. Ability. 6. Self-esteem. I. Yesh, Jeff, 1971- II. Title.

QL706.2 .B66 2013
599.362/083   2013934335

Great Books for Growing Minds
A division of Five Star Publications, Inc.

Electronic edition provided by

www.eStarPublish.com
the eDivision of Five Star Publications, Inc.

Printed in the United States of America

Cover, Illustration & Design: Jeff Yesh
Page Layout & Design: Jeff Yesh and Kris Taft Miller
Development Editor: Jennifer Steele Christensen
Curriculum Guide Writers: Jean Kilker and Jennifer Steele Christensen
Proofreader: Cristy Bertini
Project Manager: Patti Crane

This Book Belongs to:

Dedications

To Willie and Rudy Bommersbach and their beautiful,
squirrel-friendly backyard.

-Jana Bommersbach

For my wife, Lori, and our daughters, Keira and Hanna.
Also, "Nuts" the squirrel.

-Jeff Yesh

This Squirrel's Story is based on a true tale witnessed in the
spring of 2007 by Rudy and Willie Bommersbach in their
backyard in Hankinson, North Dakota.

The first thing you need to know is that squirrels don't live in birdhouses.

I should know. My name is Shirlee, and I'm a squirrel.

So, how did I end up raising my babies in a birdhouse in the backyard of a nice man and woman in North Dakota?

That's the story I'm going to tell you. It all started with a big, fat, black cat. I don't know where she came from, but one day, there she was—the biggest, fattest, **meanest-looking** cat I had ever seen. From the minute we laid eyes on each other, I knew she was licking her whiskers.

"Catch me if you can," I teased. I scampered up a tree as fast as I could—climbing much higher than this overweight cat could ever climb. I knew it made her mad that she was stuck on the ground while I was laughing at her from above. I could have jumped from branch to branch to get even farther away, but to be honest, it was fun to sit there and watch that helpless cat meow her head off at me.

I don't speak cat, *but if I did*, I'd bet that fat feline was saying, "Mrs. Squirrel, you're going to be my supper one of these days."

That thought worried me. So, from
that day on, I watched very carefully
for that black cat. I started thinking,
What if she finds my nest when I have my
babies? They will be so little at first. They'll be
blind and helpless. They wouldn't be able to get
away from her.

I knew I had to find the safest nest ever to protect
my children. What should I do?

I was wondering just that when the nice man came out of his house carrying a beautiful, very safe-looking birdhouse.

By then, I'd watched this man a lot. He was very big! At first, his size scared me, but the more I watched him, the more I saw that he was kind.

Every spring, I watched him plant a big garden and I learned that he relied on the nice woman as his "go-fer." He'd ask for something, and she'd "go for" it right away. He'd ask for something else, and she'd go for that, too. The woman always helped the man all she could.

All winter, I watched the man keep his bird feeder full of seeds. He knew the birds had trouble finding food in all that snow and I thought it was a very nice thing for him to do. There were many days I was thankful for his generosity. I always buried seeds and nuts for my winter food, but to be honest, it was much easier some days to just climb into the feeder for a free meal. I didn't think the nice man would mind.

I liked watching him clean up the four birdhouses he'd hung in the yard. He always seemed really happy when the birds came to live in them and raise their babies. He and the nice woman would sit in their lawn chairs for hours to watch the birds. That was another good sign of how nice they were.

I don't speak people, but it didn't take me long to learn that when the woman wanted the man, she called out "Rudy." When he wanted her, he called for "Willie." Any smart squirrel would realize those had to be their names.

On the day I first started worrying about that horrible cat, I watched with great interest as Rudy brought out a splendid new birdhouse. Willie carried out a hammer and nails.

As they nailed the house to a sturdy tree at the back of the yard, I kept hearing the people words **"wood"** and **"duck."** At the time, I had no idea what a wood duck was. I'm guessing now that it was the strange, brightly colored bird that showed up several weeks later and was startled to see a mother squirrel with two new babies living in her house.

I don't speak wood duck, *but if I did*, I'd bet that bird was scolding, "What do you think you're doing in a house meant for me? Don't you know that squirrels don't live in birdhouses?"

Instead of arguing with her in squirrel, which I didn't think she'd understand, I just swatted at her with my paw until she flew away. We never had any more trouble with her after that. The birdhouse was our home, and we settled right in.

I'm proud to report I had two children. My little ones were totally different from one another. I named my girl **Sally**. She was a curious child from the beginning. She opened her eyes before her brother, she crawled around the house first, and her tail grew long and bushy first. She was eager to get going in life. I could hardly keep her inside.

I named my boy **Sammy**. He was far more timid than his sister. He didn't scamper like Sally, he didn't want to explore, and he didn't hang his head out the door to look at the big world outside. He seemed content to just rest in the clean straw bedding in our house all day. He had me worried because timid squirrels have a hard time in life, but I hoped that as he grew, his squirrel traits would show up.

Before long, I realized that my instincts about needing to find a safe place to live had been right. Soon after Sally and Sammy were born, that black cat came skulking around our house. Thankfully, she couldn't get up the tree. Even if she could have climbed up this high, she couldn't fit through the round hole that was our front door. My little ones were safe and secure as they started to grow in our cozy, wood duck house.

It was in that house that I began the children's lessons.

GRAY SQUIRREL

"You are **gray tree squirrels,**" I told them. "You have cousins—the ground squirrel and the red squirrel. You can climb to the highest branch and jump from limb to limb. You can run along the ground lickety-split with your tails held high. There is one thing that separates us from our red squirrel cousins. They are called **destructive** squirrels because they like to get inside houses and chew everything up. We don't do that. We like the out-of-doors and are called **good** squirrels."

RED SQUIRREL

Sally clapped her paws at this news. "Oh Mommy, I'm so glad we're the outdoors type. There's a great big tree I want to climb. From there, I can get on the roof of that house. Won't it be wonderful to run all over it? Sammy, we'll have such fun!"

Sammy looked up at her with big, frightened eyes. **"Way up there?"** he asked in a little voice. "You want to go way up there? It's so high, Sally. What if you fall? And there's nothing on that roof I want to see. No, I don't want to go on that roof. I don't think I want to go out there at all!"

As Sammy snuggled back into the straw and buried his nose, Sally look at me with eyes that asked, "What's wrong with my brother?"

I hugged her and whispered, "Don't worry. He'll come around." But secretly, I was worried, too.

The one thing I didn't have to teach my children was how to laugh. It came naturally to Sally. She just swished her tail and chirped three times, and it was such a happy laugh that Sammy and I joined right in.

CHIRP CHIRP

One important thing I did have to teach them was how to sound the squirrel alarm. "Make a very long chirp—the longest you can and hold your tail straight up in the air," I said. "Other squirrels will either hear you or see you, and they'll know there is danger. If you ever hear that chirp or see a tail straight up in the air, climb the nearest tree. Go as high as you can, because that long, loud chirp means that something bad is happening."

Then I told them about the mean black cat. "She is **not** a friend," I stressed. "Stay away from her." I made them promise. "She could hurt you."

I also told them about the birds. "You see those birdhouses?" I asked as we looked out our front door. "Mamma and papa birds are raising their babies in those houses, just like I'm raising you here. Now be careful, because if you get too close to those houses, the parents will dive-bomb you to scare you away. They're not being mean. They're just protecting their babies, just like I would chase away anyone who came too close to our house."

Sally nodded and said she understood. Sammy just looked at me with his big, scared eyes and said, "There are so many bad things out there. I think we should just stay in here."

"Oh Sammy, how can you be such a coward? **Start acting like a squirrel,**" his sister teased, with some meanness in her voice.

Sally's jab hurt Sammy's feelings. He dove into the straw, buried his whole head and wouldn't come out for the longest time.

"Sally, apologize to your brother," I told her.

"But Motherrrr..." she started.

"Sally, **APOLOGIZE!**" I scolded.

She did say she was sorry, but it didn't sound like she meant it.

I also taught my children about finding nuts and seeds and fruit. The nice couple, Rudy and Willie, had plenty of all three in their lush backyard that would keep us fed in the spring, summer, and fall. But I had to teach the kids the secrets about burying food for winter.

"Now, when you break open a nut with your teeth," I told them as I broke open a nut with my teeth, "you lick it or rub it on your face to put your scent on it. Then when you bury it, you can always find it. You'll be able to smell that nut as your own, even if there's a foot of snow covering it."

My babies found this amazing. I have to admit it always amazed me, too.

As we continued to learn and play together, our little family was very happy in our lovely wood duck home. Rudy and Willie looked like they were happy we were there, too. They smiled a lot when they looked right at us, and when their friends came to visit, they'd always point at our house. Then everyone would laugh, as they tried to get a glimpse of my babies.
I was glad that so many people seemed happy for us.

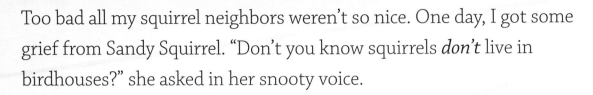

Too bad all my squirrel neighbors weren't so nice. One day, I got some grief from Sandy Squirrel. "Don't you know squirrels *don't* live in birdhouses?" she asked in her snooty voice.

I just ignored her, because keeping my babies safe was more important than what Snoopy Sandy thought. Besides, the kids and I loved our home.

I loved it all the more the day I saw Rudy take the black cat away.

I had known for a long time that Rudy and Willie didn't like the cat either. I had watched Willie yell and clap her hands to scare her away from the birdhouses. And I'd watched Rudy squirt the cat with the garden hose when he was watering. I joined him in laughing as that cat ran away as fast as she could.

One day, Rudy caught the cat, put her in a cage, and took her away in his car. When he came home, he had the cage, but not the cat. I wondered what had happened. I contacted the **SIN—Squirrel Information Network**—and their chief reporter, Steve, got back to me with good news.

"Rudy took the cat out to a farm in the country where people like having cats in their barns," he told me. "There are already several other cats there, with lots of easy mice to catch. Because they help the farmer by getting rid of the mice, he gives them fresh milk from his cows. The cats are so happy and well-fed that they almost never go after a squirrel or a bird."

You know I didn't like the cat, but I was really happy for her. She was in a nice place with other cats, and she had lots to eat. Maybe now she could be happy, too. And maybe she wouldn't be so mean anymore. Mostly I was thrilled she could no longer hurt my children. Knowing that sure helped me breathe easier!

Before long, the day finally came for my babies to leave our home and go out into the world. By now, Sally and Sammy were four times bigger than when they were born. Their eyes were clear and sharp. They had strong teeth. They had great bushy tails and lovely grayish-brown coats of fur. I thought they were the most *beautiful* squirrels ever!

Sally was more than ready to leave and go exploring. All I had to say was, "It's time," and she rushed out the front door.

Without a moment's hesitation, she climbed to the roof of the birdhouse and scampered down the tree.

"Whee!" she squealed when she reached the ground. "The grass feels so good on my paws. I love this, Mommy!"

Sally couldn't see me, but I was so happy and proud of her that I had a tear in my eye. She was going to be just fine on her own!

Sammy, on the other hand, wasn't at all interested in leaving our house. That made me want to cry, too.

"Just let me stay here," he begged. "I don't want to go outside. It's so big out there. What if I get lost? What if I can't find you? We're up so high. **What if I fall?**"

Sammy went on and on. I answered every concern, but he didn't hear me. "What if another cat comes?" he cried. "What if the birds hurt me?"

I tried to coax him. "Sammy," I said, "squirrels are natural climbers. You have nothing to worry about. Your paws have sharp nails that will hold tight to this tree. You are going to have so much fun climbing up and down. Sally's out there waiting for you. And I won't go far away. I promise."

But he was so scared, he wasn't listening.

I nudged him toward the door. Sammy poked his head out, but quickly pulled himself back in.

"I don't WANT to go out there," he protested again.

I climbed out to show him how easy it was. He peeked out again to watch me. That didn't convince him either. Back inside he ducked.

As I kept trying to persuade Sammy to come outside, I heard Rudy yell, "Willie!" She came rushing out of the house and stood next to Rudy, who was pointing at us. They both looked at us and shook their heads with a smile. They watched us all afternoon as I tried everything I could think of to get Sammy out of the house.

I bribed. I pleaded. I threatened. I even yelled. But nothing would get that boy to come out. When I reached in and tried to pull him out with my paws, he curled up in the very bottom of the house where I couldn't reach him.

Of course, I also had to keep an eye on Sally to be sure she was okay, but I didn't have to worry much. I could see she was as squirrely as a squirrel can be.

As I turned back to Sammy, I noticed that Rudy and Willie had set their lawn chairs facing our house so they could watch this scaredy-squirrel drama in style. They seemed very settled in and were enjoying glasses of tea with lots of ice.

"Sammy, I have to do this because you can't spend your whole life in this birdhouse," I told my not-so-brave boy as I climbed inside and took him in my front paws.

"Mommy, don't, Mommy, don't," he cried, as I pulled him out through the round door. I hooked my back legs on the door and stretched down toward the ground, holding Sammy tight.

I stretched as far as my body would stretch. I reached my arms as long as they would reach and held Sammy by his paws.

We dangled there for a minute.

I held my breath, closed my eyes and whispered, "You can do it, Sammy. **You can do it.**"

And then I let him go.

He landed on the ground and didn't move. He lay there motionless, and it scared me.

I saw that Rudy and Willie had jumped up from their chairs, and it looked like they were scared, too.

Oh no. I hurt him, I thought, as I started to cry.

Sammy seemed to lay there for the longest time...but looking back at it, it was really only a minute or two.

Then he stood up and gave himself a little shake. He took a timid step, and then he started running! **My boy was running!**

"Oh Mommy, Sally's right, **this grass feels so good!**" he yelled.

I was still crying, but no longer from fear. Now I had tears of joy running down my cheeks!

Sally called to him from the tree where she was perched. He ran over to her and climbed that tree like he'd done it all his life. "See, I told you it would be fun," Sally told him.

They rubbed noses, and I was so glad to see that everything was all right between my children. Sammy chirped three times and swished his tail. His laugh said it all. **"Hurray!"**

Oh, I was so relieved. My boy and girl were both safe, and Sammy had proven that he was a real squirrely squirrel after all.

I took a moment to rest and catch my breath. That's when I looked down and saw Rudy and Willie. They were still standing there, watching us. As we looked at each other, they raised their glasses to me in what I think is called a "toast."

I don't speak people, *but if I did,* I'd bet they were saying, **"You did a good job, Mamma Squirrel."**

The End

A Squirrel's Story
Curriculum Guide

Reading a story is just one of the many ways to enjoy it. Once we've been introduced to a story, we can use it to spark our own imaginations as we learn more about its subject matter and apply it to our own lives. With a parent, teacher, or other supervising grown-up, continue your own *A Squirrel's Story* adventure!

Reading

Vocabulary:

- Homonyms are words that are spelled the same way and sound the same but have different meanings. For example: Let's go to the fair. The weather is fair today.

- Homophones are words that sound the same, but are spelled differently. For example: I picked a flower. I need flour to bake cookies.

- Homographs are words that are spelled the same way but can be pronounced differently AND mean different things. For example: I am close to you. Please close the door.

Can you find examples of these types of words in the story?

READING IS FUN!

Creative Language:

A Squirrel's Story has many examples of creative language. Here are a few:

🌰 Creative adjectives using nonsense words: The phrase "lickety-split" means fast. "Squirrely" means to act like a squirrel. It can also mean to twitch and move in an unusual way.

🌰 A play on homophones: "go-fer" means "go for" and a "gopher" is a type of animal.

🌰 Dual meanings for descriptive phrasing: The cat in *A Squirrel's Story* is "licking her whiskers." Cats do this when they are hungry. "Licking their whiskers" can also be applied to people when they are anticipating something good to eat or waiting for something exciting to happen.

Can you find and explain other uses of creative language in the story?

Writing

Fiction and Nonfiction:

The term "fiction" means that a story is not true. Although there might be things in the story that could happen, they are stories that come from the author's imagination. Mysteries, fantasy, science fiction, and fairy-tales are all examples of fiction. The term "nonfiction" means that the story is true. Examples of nonfiction include biographies, autobiographies, encyclopedias, historical accounts, etc. On the title page, we learn that *A Squirrel's Story* is based on a true story. Is this story fiction or nonfiction? Justify your answer using information and words from the story.

Play a matching game

Where Do I Live?

Facts about animal habitats are considered nonfiction. Can you pair the animal with its home?

Burrow	Spider
Pond	Rabbit
Ocean	Tadpole
Desert	Earthworm
Soil	Bird
Arctic	Polar Bear
Forest	Deer
Jungle	Monkey
Nest	Coyote
Web	Whale

Next, can you create funny, fictional pairs? For example, what would happen if a whale tried to live in the desert? How would the whale have to change to live in that environment?

Write this way

Can you imitate different styles of writing?

You are a reporter who has discovered that a squirrel lives in a birdhouse.
Write a list of questions that you would ask Shirlee.
Write a list of questions that you would ask Rudy and Willie.

You are a poet.
Write a poem about the mean black cat.

- **You are a researcher.**

  Write a factual report about birdhouses. Use the Internet and/or books from the library to find out which types of birds live in which types of houses.

- **You are a student.**

  Write a journal entry for your teacher about the most interesting part of this story.

- **Tell a personal story.** Shirlee Squirrel is afraid of a big, black cat. Write a story about what you are afraid of and what helps you feel safe.

Listening

- Go outside and listen to birds chirping for 15 minutes. How many different kinds of birds did you hear? What other sounds do you hear if you live in the city? What other sounds do you hear if you live in the country?

Creating

- **Draw the cat.** What does a fat, mean, black cat look like? Cat faces are easy to draw. First, draw a circle, but not too perfectly. Next, add triangles for the ears. On the face, draw a small triangle for the nose. Off the bottom of the nose, draw a shape like an anchor to be the mouth. Depending on how curved you make it, the cat will be either smiling or sneering. Add whiskers and eyes. You can either make them round or squinted.

- **Draw a picture of your family.** Shirlee Squirrel has two children, Sammy and Sally. How many people are in **your** family? Draw a picture of your family.

- **Make a birdhouse decoration.** Make a birdhouse out of a milk carton and decorate with construction paper, wrapping paper, paint, glitter, etc. Be creative and have fun!

🌰 **Make a real birdhouse.** Rudy and Willie like to feed the birds in their backyard. With a grown-up's help, make one of these simple bird feeders for the birds that visit your own neighborhood:

- *Thread cereal with holes (Fruit Loops, Cheerios, etc.) onto a pipe cleaner, and hang it from a tree branch*
  www.notimeforflashcards.com

- *Pinecone bird feeder*
  www.busybeekidscrafts.com

- *Pretzel bird feeder*
  www.busybeekidscrafts.com

🌰 **Have a puppet show.** Use colored paper lunch bags, construction paper, markers, and crayons to make a family of squirrel hand puppets and hold a puppet show.

🌰 **Cooking.** Gray tree squirrels like to eat berries, seeds, and nuts. Do you like squirrel food? With a grown-up's help, make this yummy granola recipe:

Granola Yogurt Parfait

Ingredients:

- 2 cups vanilla yogurt
- 2 cups of your favorite granola
- 2 cups fresh berries and/or other fruit, peeled and sliced

Directions:

Line up 4 tall glasses in a row. Spoon 2 tablespoons of yogurt into each glass. Spoon 2 tablespoons of fruit over the yogurt. Spoon 2 tablespoons of granola over the fruit. **Enjoy!**

Explore Nature

Shirlee Squirrel raised her babies in author Jana Bommersbach's parents' backyard. What can you find in **your** backyard? What can you discover in the park? Enjoy your own backyard adventures!

- Go exploring with your family!
- Make a collection of the cool things you find.
- What kinds of insects/animals did you see?
- What kinds of trees and flowers grow in your neighborhood?
- If you were a squirrel, where could you find a safe home?

Learn More Online

There are many ways to learn more about squirrels. Try some of these fun activities!

Do you want to learn more about gray tree squirrels? Find out more on:

- **www.fcps.edu**
- **www.npwrc.usgs.gov**
- **www.psu.edu**

What would you say if you could speak **squirrel**? Visit **www.junglewalk.com** to hear the sounds of a gray tree squirrel.

Pretend you are a gray tree squirrel and imitate the sounds below:

- Clicking
- Chattering
- Warning

Have you ever been to North Dakota, otherwise known as the Peace Garden State? Did you know that North Dakota was once called the Flickertail State in honor of Richardson ground squirrels? These little critters are "cousins" to gray tree squirrels like Shirlee and her family. They are known for a characteristic flick of the tail that is unique to their species. Because they are so special, "The Flickertail March" is North Dakota's official state marching anthem. Visit **www.kidskonnect.com** to learn more about North Dakota.

About the Author

Jana Bommersbach

One of the Grand Canyon State's most acclaimed journalists and authors, Jana Bommersbach has been a fixture in Arizona media since the early 1970s, making an indelible mark in both broadcast and print journalism. Raised in a large extended family in North Dakota, she attended graduate school at the University of Michigan before moving to the Southwest in 1972. Named Arizona's "Journalist of the Year," she has also been honored with two lifetime achievement awards, along with multiple local, regional, and national accolades. Her first book, **The Trunk Murderess: Winnie Ruth Judd**, was a national bestseller and was named Arizona's ONEBOOKAZ for Adults selection in 2010.

Always an obedient child, Jana ventured into children's literature because her mother told her to! Living in a historic neighborhood in the heart of downtown Phoenix, she entertains the children in her life each Christmas with the annual Hoover Street Children's Party. With the introduction of **A Squirrel's Story—A True Tale**, she looks forward to entering the children's book market with gusto!

About the Illustrator
Jeff Yesh

Jeff Yesh is a freelance illustrator and graphic designer who has worked with Five Star Publications, Inc. since 2000. His award-winning work has been featured in multiple children's books including ***Last Night I Had a Laughmare*** by J.E. Laufer and ***From Seed to Apple Tree*** by Suzanne Slade. Born and raised in Indiana, Jeff graduated from Indiana State University with a bachelor of fine arts in graphic design. Based in Carmel, Indiana, Jeff enjoys being active outdoors and spending time with his wife and two daughters.

About Little Five Star
A Division of Five Star Publications, Inc.

Helping authors of children's books shape the future with great reads for growing minds...

Shining brightly since 1985, Five Star Publications, Inc. is proud of its reputation for excellence in producing and marketing award-winning books for adults and children worldwide. The genres represented in its growing collection include educational titles, nonfiction, picture books, juvenile fiction, memoirs, Westerns, novels, professional "how-to's" and more.

Having assembled a team of dozens of skilled industry professionals, Linda F. Radke, founder and president of Five Star Publications, Inc., is committed to helping both established and aspiring authors of all ages continually reach new heights. Along with providing book production/marketing services, the Five Star team also assists organizations with website redesign, logo design and corporate/product branding.

Setting the bar for partnership publishing and professionally fulfilling traditional publishing contracts, Five Star Publications is recognized as an industry leader in creativity, innovation and customer service.

Many Five Star Publications titles have been recognized on local, national and international levels, and their authors have enjoyed engaging in promotional opportunities in schools, corporations and media venues across America.

A division of Five Star Publications, Inc., Little Five Star is a proud publisher of great books for growing minds and excels in educating and entertaining young thinkers. Little Five Star helps children make better choices and accept themselves and others.

Linda F. Radke
President

www.LittleFiveStar.com

Order Form

Add these books to your Little Five Star collection!

Also available as eBooks!

ITEM	QTY	UNIT PRICE	TOTAL
A Squirrel's Story — A True Tale by Jana Bommersbach (ISBN: 978-1-58985-252-5)		$11.95 US $12.95 CAN	
Arizona Way Out West & Wacky: Awesome Activities, Humorous History and Fun Facts! by Conrad J. Storad and Lynda Exley (ISBN: 978-1-58985-047-7)		$11.95 US $12.95 CAN	
Cheery: the true adventures of a Chiricahua Leopard Frog by Elizabeth W. Davidson (ISBN: 978-1-58985-025-5)		$15.95 US $16.95 CAN	
GQ GQ. Where Are You? Adventures of a Gambel's Quail by Sharon I. Ritt (ISBN: 978-1-58985-223-5)		$14.95 US $15.95 CAN	
The Moon Saw It All by Nancy L. Young (ISBN: 978-1-58985-250-1)		$11.95 US $12.95 CAN	
Rattlesnake Rules (paperback) by Conrad J. Storad (ISBN: 978-1-58985-211-2)		$7.95 US/CAN	
		Subtotal	
*8.8% sales tax – on all orders originating in Arizona.		TAX	
* $8.00 or 10% of the total order – whichever is greater. Ground shipping. Allow 1 to 2 weeks for delivery.		Shipping	
Mail form to: Five Star Publications, Inc. PO Box 6698, Chandler, AZ 85246-6698		**TOTAL**	

NAME:

ADDRESS:

CITY, STATE, ZIP

DAY TIME PHONE NUMBER: FAX:

EMAIL:

Method of Payment:
☐ VISA ☐ MasterCard ☐ Discover Card ☐ American Express

account number ▲   expiration date ▲

signature ▲   3-4 digit security number ▲

Great Books for Growing Minds
A Division of Five Star Publications, Inc.

P.O. Box 6698 • Chandler, AZ 85246-6698
(480) 940-8182 (866) 471-0777 Fax: (480) 940-8787
info@FiveStarPublications.com
www.FiveStarPublications.com

"I enjoyed your Squirrels! I could go on and on about the real life naturalist appeal of your story. This charming story is loaded with wisdom and nature-lore for children and the adults who are lucky enough to read it to them."

—*Terry Goddard, former Phoenix Mayor and Arizona Attorney General*

"Jana Bommersbach's insightful squirrel story, beautifully illustrated by Jeff Yesh, is pure fun. Put me down for 300 books. I can hardly wait to see Jana inspire our students at her first KidsRead Family Book Breakfast."

—*Eileen Bailey, Founder/President, KidsRead, Phoenix, AZ*